Ann Kerns

Twenty-First Century Books
Minneapolis

Text copyright © 2007 by Lerner Publications Company

Twenty-First Century Books
A division of Lerner Publishing Group
241 First Avenue North
Minneapolis, MN 55401 U.S.A.

Website addresses: www.lernerbooks.com
www.biography.com

Library of Congress Cataloging-in-Publication Data

Kerns, Ann.
   Martha Stewart / by Ann Kerns.
     p.   cm. — (Biography)
   Includes bibliographical references and index.
   ISBN-13: 978–0–8225–6613–7 (lib. bdg. : alk. paper)
   ISBN-10: 0–8225–6613–3 (lib. bdg. : alk. paper)
     1. Stewart, Martha—Juvenile literature. 2. Home economists—United States—Biography—Juvenile literature. 3. Businesswomen—United States—Biography—Juvenile literature. I. Title. II. Series: Biography (Twenty-First Century Books)
   TX140.S74K47 2007
   640.92—dc22   2006005067

Manufactured in the United States of America
1 2 3 4 5 6 – BP – 12 11 10 09 08 07

CONTENTS

Stewart and her daughter, Alexis, walk to a chartered plane after Stewart's release from prison. Stewart is wearing a hand-knit poncho, a gift from one of her fellow inmates.

INTRODUCTION

Just after midnight on March 4, 2005, Martha Stewart slipped out a side door. She headed directly for one of two chauffeur-driven sports utility vehicles (SUVs). Wearing a hand-knit gray and white poncho, jeans, and heeled boots, sixty-four-year-old Stewart looked young and slim. As soon as she was inside the SUV, both vehicles sped to a nearby airport. There a chartered jet waited on a runway.

Stewart—a woman who had had a television program, a magazine, and a line of home products all bearing her name—did not slip out the side door of a glamorous party. She was not trying to escape the news photographers known as paparazzi. She was not headed home from a date at a luxury restaurant. Stewart, a symbol of elegant, upscale living, was being released from prison.

For five months, Stewart had been an inmate at Alderson Federal Prison Camp in Alderson, West Virginia. In March 2004, she was found guilty of obstruction of justice—of lying to federal authorities. The authorities had been investigating the legality of Stewart's sale of some stock market shares.

After her release from Alderson, Stewart was ordered by the court to serve another five months under house arrest. Except for forty-eight hours a week, she was not allowed to leave her home. And those forty-eight free hours were meant only for certain activities, such as work, grocery shopping, and doctor appointments. At all times, Stewart was required to wear a monitoring device around her ankle, which court authorities used to track her location.

Stewart's stay at Alderson could not be considered "hard time." Alderson is a minimum-security prison for women, many of whom are convicted of nonviolent crimes. Tucked away in the West Virginia countryside, it is known jokingly as Camp Cupcake. And Stewart's house arrest may seem mild too. The house in question is a $16 million mansion on a 153-acre estate.

But Stewart's conviction and imprisonment were more than personal drama. They represented the possible downfall of a billionaire business genius. Stewart was a powerful woman in command of an entire media empire. At the time of her arrest in 2002, her company, Martha Stewart Living Omnimedia (MSLO), was worth $11.8 million. It employed almost six hundred people in six states and had operations in Canada and Japan.

Stewart's release raised many questions. Could she— or should she—become an executive of her company again? Her crime had damaged the company's reputation, putting her stockholders' money and her employees' jobs at risk. In allowing her to resume leadership, was her company sending the message that it was okay to be a criminal, as long as you were rich? And was Stewart's image so tarnished that no public relations campaign, no matter how skillful, could return its shine?

Or was Stewart, as she had always claimed, innocent of the crime for which she had been imprisoned? Was she the victim of eager government investigators? In the past few years, financial scandals involving the management of several large U.S. companies had made headlines in the national news. By going after Stewart, were government officials just anxious to look as though they were clamping down on corporate crime?

Stewart's imprisonment and return to public life were controversial. But Stewart is no stranger to controversy. She has always had strong supporters and equally strong critics. Social issues such as modern home life, corporate greed, and the public versus the private life of a celebrity seem to swirl around any discussion of Stewart. But even her enemies admit that she is a phenomenal, self-made success. The journey that brought Stewart such fame and fortune has been a long one, with a very humble beginning.

Jersey City, New Jersey, in the early 1940s

Chapter **ONE**

AN EARLY ACHIEVER

MARTHA STEWART WAS BORN MARTHA HELEN Kostyra on August 3, 1941. When she was born, her parents, Edward and Martha, and her three-year-old brother, Eric, were living in a small apartment in Jersey City, New Jersey. Just ten miles across the Hudson River from New York City, Jersey City was a working-class town. Edward was a high school gym teacher. Martha had been a grade-school teacher until Eric was born. Like many Jersey City residents, Edward and Martha were first-generation Americans. Both were the children of Polish immigrants.

When little Martha was three years old, the family moved about eight miles away to the town of Nutley, New Jersey. Nutley is a middle-class suburb of

Newark, New Jersey's largest city. It is a town of tree-lined streets, old stone churches, parks, and family-owned shops.

LIFE IN NUTLEY

One of the main industries in Nutley was pharmaceuticals, companies that develop and sell drugs to hospitals and pharmacies. Edward got a job as a pharmaceutical salesperson. His new job required him to commute to New York City almost every day. He often traveled around New Jersey too. Edward had a busy schedule, but the pay was much better than he had earned as a gym teacher. He and his wife purchased a modest house on Elm Street. The house's

Martha grew up in this Dutch Colonial home on Elm Street in Nutley, New Jersey.

three bedrooms were soon filled with four more children—Frank, Kathy, George, and Laura.

The Kostyras' move to Nutley paralleled the experience of families across the United States at that time. The late 1940s and early 1950s were the height of the baby boom, the population explosion that followed the end of World War II (1939–1945). Americans felt relieved that the war was over. They were optimistic about the future. Post-war business and industry in the United States grew quickly. Finding a secure, good-paying job was relatively easy, and the white middle class expanded. For the first time since the 1930s, people began marrying younger and having more children. Many of these young couples could afford to leave their cramped city apartments. They moved to the suburbs into single-family homes with large garages for their new cars.

As a result of the baby boom, the streets of towns such as Nutley were filled with children. Schools had to add annexes or build new, larger schools to accommodate the overflow of students. Outside of school, these baby boomer kids had more free time and more spending money of their own than kids of the past. In Nutley the children fished at the Mud Hole in summer and skated on it in winter. They enjoyed New Jersey's famous Brookdale sodas at the Candy Corner and spent their allowances on record albums at the five-and-dime store. Friday night football games at Nutley High School drew big crowds. And *It's a Wonderful Life, Red River,* and *Father of the Bride* played at the Franklin Theater.

HELPING AROUND THE HOUSE

The Kostyra children, too, enjoyed all these activities. But they were a close-knit family, and more often they spent their free time at home. Gathered around the kitchen table, the Kostyras played card games or the word game Scrabble. They did not have a television, so they listened to the radio. Radio programs such as *Ozzie and Harriet*, a family comedy, and *The Lone Ranger*, a western adventure show, were favorites.

Although their financial situation had improved, Edward and Martha still did not have much money. Both parents were hardworking and tried to trim household expenses by doing things themselves. Mrs. Kostyra made all the children's clothes on her sewing machine. Edward did most of the repairs around the house.

Edward also planted a large garden in the backyard. The yard was only fifty feet wide, and it sloped down steeply from the house. But Edward made the best use of the space. He created terraces, flat areas built like large steps into the slopes. He grew vegetables on the upper terrace and fruit trees and flowers on the lower terrace. He also grew some vegetables in part of a large vacant lot at the end of the yard. Edward's gardens yielded more than enough vegetables and fruit for the family. What was leftover, Mrs. Kostyra preserved and canned.

In a small house with a large family, there were many daily chores. Organization and discipline were important to the Kostyras. As the eldest girl, Martha was expected to do more than the other children. She learned to help her father in the garden when she was still a toddler. A few years later, she was helping Edward choose vegetables from his many seed catalogs. He taught her how to start plants indoors in the early spring, planting the seeds in the bottoms of milk cartons.

Martha also helped her mother clean, do laundry, and take care of the younger children. She learned to sew her own clothes. And at a time when most children are not allowed to use the stove, Martha learned to cook. When she was eight, her parents gave her a cookbook with simple recipes. Martha tried every one. Her favorite was the recipe for butterscotch candy. Martha's mother also taught her how to make many traditional Polish dishes, such as pierogi (dumplings stuffed with cabbage and meat).

Next door to the Kostyras lived the Mauses, a German immigrant couple. The Mauses had worked as professional bakers. Although they were retired, they had kept much of their professional equipment. They set up a baking kitchen in their basement with commercial ovens, huge mixing bowls, and large metal baking sheets. The Kostyra kids all enjoyed being taste testers for the Mauses' daily assortment of breads, strudels, coffeecakes, pies, and tarts.

Martha wanted to do more than taste the results. Mrs. Maus began allowing Martha to help knead bread dough. Mrs. Maus taught her to bake cherry and peach pies made with fresh fruit from the backyard trees.

Martha also learned housekeeping tips from her maternal grandparents, the Ruszkowskis. The Ruszkowskis lived in Buffalo, a town in upstate New York. Martha loved to spend summer days there picking cherries, peaches, and strawberries. After all the fruit was picked, her grandmother, Franciska, would show Martha how to can the fruits to preserve them, just as she had taught Martha's mother.

Too Little Childhood?

Martha has often credited these experiences with setting her on the road to fortune as a cooking and crafting adviser. She and her siblings have remarked that Martha actually enjoyed baking, cooking, and gardening more than she enjoyed playing dolls or games. Martha also admired her parents' can-do attitude. In many of her magazine columns, she writes with pride of the care and time they put into everything. And she often praises the virtues of tradition, of the handmade and the home cooked over the store bought.

But some Stewart biographers have suggested that Edward and Martha Kostyra's need for order and discipline was not reasonable in a house full of growing kids. Edward, it has been argued, wanted everything done his way and on his schedule. Some of the people who grew up in Martha's Nutley neighborhood also remember Edward as very stern and unpleasant. They recall steering well clear of the Kostyra house when he was out in the yard.

Martha has admitted that her father was a "total perfectionist." In a television interview, she related how she and her siblings were expected to help her father with household repairs. "We all stood there like nurses at an operation, and we just stood there and waited until my dad said, 'Hand me the Phillips head screwdriver,' and we had to know what a Phillips head screwdriver was."

But Martha defends both her parents' attitudes. "[A]t home we were always told, you can do anything you want. You can be anything you want," she said. "I think the nicest thing a parent can tell a kid is that you just don't have any limits."

Martha was Edward's favorite child, and she tried hard to win his approval. She did all her chores well and was obedient at home. She also put her parents' can-do spirit to work at school. Martha was a straight-A student, well rounded in math, science, and art. Even after more than forty years, some of Martha's school friends could recall how outstanding her art projects were.

Martha's sister Kathy remarked in an interview that going to school was the first time she realized her family was different. Other kids did not wear homemade clothes. Their families had cars and television sets. Their mothers had automatic washers and dryers, and they bought their food at the new supermarkets that sprang up in every suburb. And the kids did not have so many chores and duties. "I think we could all see the differences between families who had more," Kathy said.

But Martha was less embarrassed than Kathy by her family's routines. For her, family life and school blended together as places to learn. Martha loved gathering new information and finding new ways to use it. And, as at home, Martha gravitated toward the adults at school. She was, she admits, a teacher's pet. "I felt that when you learned from your teacher. . . if you're working by the teacher's side, you are going to learn more than anybody else." By the time Martha left grade school, her drive and independence were set.

High School

Martha entered Nutley High School in 1955. She was pretty, with delicate features, soft blonde hair, and a slim, athletic figure. Martha had a few male friends, but she did not date much. And she did not mind. For Martha, high school was all about preparing for college. She knew she had ambition and strength. But to get ahead, Martha would have to learn how to focus those qualities.

In a 2000 interview, television host Oprah Winfrey and Martha discussed "owning themselves." By this they meant taking control of and taking responsibility for what happens to them. "When did you start to take ownership of your life?" Winfrey asked. Martha answered without hesitation: "In high school."

To prepare for college, Martha took difficult classes in math and science. She was the first girl at Nutley High School to take advanced math. Martha also enjoyed reading—often far beyond the level of her classmates. She loved the novels of American authors Edith Wharton, Willa Cather, and Upton Sinclair. She also enjoyed Russian literature, such as the novels of Leo Tolstoy, Fyodor Dostoevsky, and Nikolay Gogol.

Martha also joined many school clubs, including the Gym Club, the Latin Club, and the Art Club. She worked on the school newspaper and volunteered as a Red Cross helper. Martha liked learning new things and being with her classmates during club activities. But her extracurricular activities were also important for her academic record. She counted on them and her excellent grades to get her into a good college.

MARTHA'S FAVORITE READING

ne of Martha's favorite novels in high school was *Anna Karenina* by Leo Tolstoy. Tolstoy's heroine, Anna, is a strong-willed woman in nineteenth-century Russia. Her search for happiness brings her to a tragic end. Another of Martha's favorites was Willa Cather's novel *My Antonia*. Martha admired the spirit and hard work of the story's immigrant pioneers on the Nebraska prairie.

Martha was involved in many extracurricular activities in high school. Here, she poses with the honor society. Martha is at the far right in the first row.

Edward and Martha supported their daughter's academic ambitions. They were very proud that Martha was planning on higher education. But Martha understood that, with six children, her parents could not afford to pay for her college tuition. Martha knew that if she wanted to go to college, she would have to get there on her own. To build up her own savings, Martha worked when she was not in school or helping at home. She babysat for neighborhood children for fifty cents an hour. On the weekends, she sold hot dogs at high school football games.

FIRST CAREER

In 1958, when Martha was starting her junior year, she discovered that a neighbor was modeling for catalogs and newspaper and magazine advertisements. Martha knew she was pretty. She also photographed well and had good taste in clothes. She wondered if she could make money as a model too.

To audition for modeling jobs, Martha needed a portfolio, or a set of sample photographs. Modeling agencies use portfolios to judge whether someone photographs well and has poise. Edward helped his daughter prepare her portfolio. He also used some of his business contacts in New York City to find Martha an agent. An agent is someone who arranges auditions and takes care of legal issues, such as signing job contracts. Within weeks Martha was looking for—and getting—modeling work in Manhattan, the business center of New York City.

Martha had the blonde, athletic, all-American looks that were popular at the time. She began appearing in catalogs for department stores and in magazine ads for Breck and Clairol shampoo and for Taryton cigarettes. She even appeared in a TV ad, mowing the lawn with an equally blond and athletic young man, to promote Lifebuoy soap.

On Saturdays Martha modeled dresses at Bonwit Teller, an upscale department store in Manhattan. At the time, large department stores held regular fashion shows to display new women's clothing. Although she was just seventeen, Martha could look quite sophisticated. With smoky eye shadow, dark lipstick, and tailored clothes, Martha looked like a twenty-something Manhattan career woman.

This photo of Martha appeared in the February 20, 1959, Nutley High School newspaper. The picture was part of a front-page story called "Photogenic Senior Makes T.V. Spots a Pleasure."

Whatever role she played—blonde teenager or well-dressed Manhattanite—modeling paid off for Martha. In her first year, she regularly made fifteen dollars an hour. That was more than many adults made in office jobs. Her modeling fees added quite a bit more to her college fund than babysitting and hot dog vending had done.

LEAVING NUTLEY

In 1959, her senior year, Martha was awarded a full scholarship to New York University (NYU) in Manhattan. She also won a partial scholarship to Barnard College, also in Manhattan. Although NYU offered her more money, Martha chose Barnard. In her interviews at Barnard, she liked the students and faculty she met. She also liked the fact that Barnard was a small college but was located in a large city. Barnard was a prestigious school, and Martha was excited and nervous about her choice.

Edward believed his daughter was going places, and he urged her to leave Nutley High School with a bang. With his encouragement, Martha chaired the decorations committee for the senior class prom. She and Edward designed and created a decorations scheme called Stairway to the Stars. The theme featured tinseled clouds hanging from the ceiling of the high school gym. Prom couples climbed up a winding white staircase to have their pictures taken.

Her classmates were awed by the elaborate decorations and by Martha's imagination and skill. "It was beautifully done," recalls Michael Geltrude, one of Martha's high school friends. Martha was pleased that the prom was a success. But in many ways, her thoughts were no longer with Nutley High School. She was already looking ahead to the bright lights of the big city.

Martha at Barnard College

Chapter **TWO**

OFF TO MANHATTAN

MARTHA KOSTYRA BEGAN ATTENDING BARNARD college in the fall of 1959. Barnard is a private women's college on the Upper West Side of Manhattan. The college is part of a large city neighborhood that includes Columbia University, the Manhattan School of Music, and other academic institutions. Famous Barnard alumnae include anthropologist Margaret Mead, novelist Zora Neale Hurston, and comedian Joan Rivers. Kostyra's class included future choreographer Twyla Tharp and future novelist Erica Jong.

With a partial scholarship, Kostyra still had many expenses. She had to pay the remainder of her tuition and buy books and supplies. With those expenses, she could not afford to live on campus or rent an apartment in Manhattan. So Kostyra lived at home and took the bus from Nutley to Barnard every morning.

Barnard draws students from across the United States and from forty other countries. Many of Kostyra's classmates came from wealthy U.S. and European families. These young women were mature, sophisticated, and had few worries about how to pay for clothes and apartments. Kostyra felt a little in awe of her wealthy friends at first. She was insecure about her homemade dresses and her daily bus trips back and forth to New Jersey.

But soon Kostyra was more interested than awed. She was impressed by her classmates' self-confidence and social skills. They moved with ease through classes and campus activities. They knew how to make small talk at parties and which forks to use at dinner. Kostyra also noted that the most attractive young women dressed with their own sense of style. They were creative with colors, jewelry, and scarves, yet they always looked perfectly put together.

Kostyra planned to study chemistry at Barnard. But in her studies, Kostyra found herself more drawn to style and creativity than to chemistry. Soon after arriving at Barnard, she switched her major course of study from science to art, European history, and architectural history.

Kostyra continued to model after classes to help pay the bills. Like Barnard, her modeling exposed her to creative and stylish people. As she matured, more important clients hired her to model. This introduced her to a whole new level of photographers, designers, and other models. The people she met at this time in her life were very different from her friends back in Nutley. "It certainly expanded my horizons," Kostyra said.

Classes and work kept her very busy, and the modeling money gave her a sense of independence. She seemed to thrive on her packed schedule. She loved her art and architecture classes, and the glamour of life in Manhattan intrigued and impressed her.

A New Love

In 1961, Kostyra's sophomore year at Barnard, she moved out of her parents' house to Manhattan. She got a job as a live-in helper for two elderly sisters. The sisters lived in a twelve-room apartment on Fifth Avenue. Before and after class, Kostyra cooked, cleaned, and shopped for her employers. In exchange for her work, Kostyra lived rent free in the housekeeper's rooms at the back of the apartment.

She appreciated the work and having a nice place to live in expensive Manhattan. But Kostyra often felt as if she were back at home tied to her parents' endless routine of household chores. She was determined to forge ahead with her modeling career and to make enough money to be truly independent.

That year Kostyra heard about a contest being held by *Glamour* magazine. Every year *Glamour* put out a special issue showcasing fashionable young women attending colleges in the United States. Kostyra believed that winning a spot in that issue would bring her more modeling work. She sent in photographs of herself and a few weeks later learned that she had won. Kostyra's photograph and a short biography appeared in *Glamour*'s Ten Best Dressed College Girls issue of 1961.

Getting her picture in a popular national magazine was not the only exciting thing happening in Kostyra's life. She had met a young man named Andrew Stewart. Andy, as he was called, was twenty-three. He was a law school student at Yale University in New Haven, Connecticut. New Haven is about seventy-five miles from Manhattan. Andy's sister Dianne attended Barnard with Kostyra, and she had set up the pair on a blind date.

Kostyra had never had a serious boyfriend, but her relationship with Andy quickly deepened. Andy was six feet tall and handsome. As a "Yalie" and a future lawyer, he made quite an impression on Kostyra. Beyond that, she admired his honesty and his serious attitude. Most college boys, Kostyra felt, were immature and silly. Andy seemed much more grown-up. But he was also warm and fun to be with. The couple enjoyed their time together socializing at Yale and Barnard dances, exploring Manhattan, and visiting each other's families.

1960s Fashion

n the 1940s and 1950s, high school and college girls often wore simple white blouses, cardigan sweaters, and skirts. They also usually wore short white socks and flat shoes, earning them the nickname bobby-soxers. Fashion magazines and designers did not bother much with the bobby-soxers. They directed their attention instead to older women with money to spend.

But as baby boomers grew into fashion consumers, magazines and designers began to cater to younger styles. One youthful influence on fashion came from an unlikely source: the White House. In 1960 John F. Kennedy was the youngest man ever elected U.S. president. His wife, Jacqueline (Jackie) Kennedy, was also young and attractive, and she became a media sensation. Looking back, Jackie's fashion sense is called elegant and classic. But in her day, she was a youthful trendsetter, especially in the stuffy confines of the White House.

Jackie Kennedy was a style icon in the 1960s.

Another influence on youth fashion in the 1960s was the mod look from Great Britain. Across Europe and the United States, young people began wearing mod items such as knee-high leather boots; fitted suede coats; short, straight skirts; chunky jewelry; and brightly patterned pantyhose.

1960s fashion model Twiggy shows off the popular mod style.

THE ORIGINAL
MARTHA STEWART WEDDING

Within months Martha and Andy had fallen in love and were planning a future together. "I never expected that," Kostyra said, but it was "exciting." In the spring of Kostyra's sophomore year, the couple became engaged.

Together they announced their plans to their parents. Andy's parents, George and Ethel, were surprised by the news—and not altogether happy. George was a stock market investor, and the family lived well in Manhattan. But Martha's humble New Jersey background was not what concerned the Stewarts. They both liked Martha. Their concern was that she was only nineteen years old. Couldn't the couple wait?

Kostyra and Andy heard a similar argument at the Kostyra home. Edward and Martha were so proud of their straight-A, scholarship-winning daughter. They wanted her to concentrate on her studies and graduate with honors. When Kostyra explained that she would not be going back to Barnard in the fall, her parents were very upset.

The decision also shocked Kostyra's friends at Barnard. They thought of themselves as part of a new generation of young women, well educated and destined for careers. "We believed that we could run the world," said Ariadney Clifton, a Barnard classmate. None of them, Clifton explained, expected to be housewives. Kostyra assured her friends that she would return to get her degree as soon as Andy finished law school. But it still seemed to her friends that Kostyra was derailing her academic career while Andy gave up nothing.

Not everyone shared these worries about the marriage. Kathy, Kostyra's fifteen-year-old sister, was almost as excited by the engagement as the couple was. "They were great together," Kathy says. She recalls that Andy, for all his impressive education and family background, was right at home in the modest house on Elm Street. He could comfortably plop on the living room sofa or join in a board game at the kitchen table.

Kostyra and Andy listened to their parents' concerns, but they would not give up their plans to be married as soon as possible. Kostyra began planning a wedding for the coming summer. It would be a small affair, with few expenses. Only close family members and a few friends would be invited.

Kostyra and her mother began work on the wedding dress. The white gown was made of organdy, a finely woven cotton fabric. It was embroidered all over with small daisies. Kostyra bought a small hat known as a pillbox and added a short net veil. Kathy, the maid of honor, and the other bridesmaids would wear silk dresses.

On the morning of the wedding, July 1, 1961, Ethel gave Kostyra a bouquet of daisies to match her dress. Then Kostyra and Andy were married in Saint Paul's

The Stewarts were married in Saint Paul's Chapel, above, at Columbia University.

Chapel at Columbia University. Martha Kostyra became Martha Stewart. After the ceremony, the families and guests enjoyed a simple lunch in the Barberry Room of Manhattan's Berkshire Hotel.

NEWLYWEDS

The newlyweds did not take a honeymoon. Instead, they packed up Martha's things and set out for New Haven. They wanted to settle in before Andy had to return to classes in the fall. They rented a house with another young married couple at Yale while Andy finished law school.

Many couples learn a lot about each other in their first year of marriage. Some sources have suggested that one of the things Stewart learned concerned Andy's family. The Stewarts were not as wealthy as she had believed. Nothing indicates that Andy lied about the issue to his wife. More likely, Stewart just assumed the family was rich.

With their trips to Europe, their suites at expensive Manhattan residential hotels, and their beachside vacation house, the Stewarts certainly lived like millionaires. But in reality, George Stewart had lost as much money in the stock market as he had made. Their finances were actually very shaky, and they could contribute very little to help the young couple. So Martha Stewart returned to modeling to help pay expenses.

In June 1962, Andy graduated from Yale Law School. The couple moved back to New York City. They rented a small, cheap apartment on the Upper West Side of Manhattan. Stewart returned to Barnard to finish her degree. Andy got a part-time job doing research for a law firm. He also began studying for a master of law degree from Columbia.

For the next two years, the couple did very little except study and work. But in 1964, they got their rewards. Stewart graduated from Barnard with a bachelor of arts degree in European history and architecture. And Andy finished his master's degree.

HONEYMOON IN EUROPE

To celebrate their achievements, the couple took a delayed honeymoon to Europe. The summer after they graduated, they toured France, Greece, and Italy. Still financially strapped, the couple aimed to spend only five dollars a day. To keep expenses down, they avoided long stays in Paris, Rome, and other big cities. Instead, they toured the countries' back roads and stayed at small family-owned inns and pensions (houses with rooms to rent).

In avoiding tourist hotels and fancy restaurants, the Stewarts found themselves having fun and interesting experiences. They chatted with the innkeepers and local people, shopped at small markets, and learned of offbeat things to do.

Both Stewart and Andy were struck by the charming inns, cottages, and cafés in rural France and Italy. Country French and Tuscan Italian decorating styles have become common in the United States. But that

Stewart and Andy fell in love with the charming inns of the Italian countryside.

was not so in the 1960s. To Stewart in particular, it was very new, yet very old-fashioned. Local crafts and food reminded her of how her family still treasured some of its Polish traditions.

With her excellent academic background, Stewart enjoyed all the history and architecture that could be found in even the smallest villages. But she also found herself soaking up the decorating styles of the inns and homes. She made notes of fabrics, tiles, and furniture.

She and Andy both enjoyed the simple but delicious food they were served. Dishes all varied by regions, Stewart learned, as people cooked with fresh, local ingredients. Whenever possible, Stewart quizzed her hosts or café chefs on how each dish was prepared. She wanted to be able to cook them herself once she got back home.

SETTLING DOWN

After their honeymoon, Stewart and Andy returned to New York City. Andy began a new job at a Manhattan law firm. Stewart began modeling full-time. The couple could afford to leave their tiny student apartment behind. They rented a much larger apartment on Riverside Drive, a wide thoroughfare that overlooks the Hudson River.

The new apartment was spacious and comfortable. But the couple had nothing with which to fill the rooms. They had only cheap student furniture and dishes. In decorating their new home, Stewart and Andy wanted to find things of value and beauty.

Both knew they wanted to re-create the charming, traditional interiors they had seen in Europe. They began to scour auctions, antique stores, and flea markets on the weekends. They looked for furniture, lamps, vases, and paintings.

In order to understand what she was buying—and to avoid overpaying—Stewart studied furniture design and quality. She learned how to determine the market value of antiques and how to tell originals from modern copies. Some of the furniture purchased at auctions and flea markets was not in good shape. Pieces had to be repaired or have their paint finish restored. So Stewart and Andy learned furniture restoration too. Family members worried that the young couple was living beyond their means. But the Stewarts were determined to make their apartment a showcase.

Stewart still loved gardening. She fondly recalled helping her father in the backyard in Nutley. But for most people in the crowded neighborhoods of Manhattan, gardening is limited to growing a few flowers in window boxes. The Stewarts, however, were different. They often took weekend drives in the country. Sometimes Stewart picked armloads of wildflowers out in the fields. Other times she bought fresh flowers from roadside farm stands or local plant nurseries. Back in their city apartment, she filled vases for every room. She also grew herbs in flowerpots in the kitchen.

Decorating, antiquing, and trips to the country kept the Stewarts busy on weekends. But Stewart had not forgotten about her dream to re-create the food she and Andy had tasted in Europe. She bought a copy of *Mastering the Art of French Cooking* by Julia Child. Child was an American chef who had studied cooking in Paris. Her 750-page cookbook was wildly popular in the United States. Child's motto was, "If you can read, you can cook." Stewart took that advice. She

COOKS OF A FEATHER

As a young wife, Martha Stewart was inspired by Julia Child's *Mastering the Art of French Cooking*. She may not have known it at the time, but Stewart had several things in common with Child. Like Stewart, Child attended a prestigious women's school on the East Coast. She graduated from Smith College in Massachusetts in 1934 with a degree in history. Child also knew nothing about French cooking until she went to France with her husband. As with Stewart, tasting French food and seeing how the French served meals inspired Child. She decided to bring the art of gourmet cooking to Americans. She included recipes, instructions, and advice on how to buy everything from copper pots to fresh broccoli. She wrote many cookbooks. Her long-running television show, *The French Chef*, began in 1963. Until her death in 2004, Child was the doyenne—the most expert and experienced woman—of television chefs.

read Child's book cover to cover. Then she began cooking. Her goal was to make every recipe in the book at least once.

Early in 1965, the Stewarts learned that they had one more decorating task ahead of them. They needed to set up a nursery. The couple was expecting a baby, due the following fall.

LEXI

Alexis Gilbert Stewart was born on September 27, 1965. She was a pretty, healthy baby, and the Stewarts were thrilled. "I'll never forget how excited and joyous she was to have this baby," Kathy recalls of her sister. The Stewarts called their new daughter Lexi for short.

The Stewarts wanted a weekend retreat from New York City. They wanted Lexi to enjoy some fresh air and nature. They also wanted to pursue their own interests in remodeling and gardening. So just one month after Lexi was born, Stewart and Andy bought an old one-room schoolhouse in Middlefield, Massachusetts. The school sat on fifty acres of wooded land in the foothills of the Berkshire Mountains.

The Berkshire Mountains are in western Massachusetts, close to the border with New York State. The area is known for its beautiful mountain peaks, quiet rivers, and old forests. Many of the towns that dot the hillsides and valleys have steepled churches and eighteenth-century colonial buildings. Much of the area is rustic and quaint, making it a favorite destination for campers and nature lovers.

The Stewarts' schoolhouse, built in 1890, was quite rustic itself. It had no plumbing and no heating. For warmth, the Stewarts relied on a fireplace and a pot-bellied stove. Both units required Stewart and Andy to chop and haul wood. They also had to carry water from a mountain stream almost one-half mile away.

For some people, this would be more work than relaxation. But the Stewarts loved their rural getaway. With Lexi in tow, Stewart and Andy gathered mushrooms in the surrounding woods and picked wild blueberries and strawberries. They repaired and painted the schoolhouse and planted a vegetable garden. With their first crop, Stewart won ribbons at the county fair for her cabbages, cauliflowers, and tomatoes.

The Stewarts loved the isolation of their Berkshire retreat. But they also enjoyed the social life in New York City. What was the point of having a showcase apartment if you never showed it off? And why learn to cook delicious gourmet French meals if you never had dinner guests? The Stewarts began having friends and coworkers over regularly for cocktail and dinner parties. Their guests marveled at the Stewart's beautiful furniture and lavish meals. Some wondered how the young couple could afford everything. But the parties were always a success. Their first Christmas party, with beautiful decorations and many kinds of homemade cookies, was such fun that it became an annual tradition.

The Stewarts enjoyed rural life. Here, Andy holds one of their hens, a black Cochin.

Chapter THREE

EARLY CAREER

IN 1967, WHEN LEXI WAS TWO YEARS OLD, STEWART decided to return to work. She hoped to continue modeling. But she had been out of the business for a while, and her career had lost some momentum. And as a twenty-five-year-old mother, Stewart no longer exactly fit the profile of the era's young, hip, carefree models. She found few modeling job offers coming her way.

Stewart realized that she needed a new career. She wanted something high paying and exciting, but what? She turned to her father-in-law for advice. George suggested that she try her hand as a stockbroker, someone who buys and sells stock market shares for clients. She was smart and ambitious.

And lots of new stockbrokerage companies were popping up on Wall Street in Lower Manhattan, home of the New York Stock Exchange (NYSE). Once, older, wealthy men had ruled Wall Street. But opportunities for younger men and women were opening up.

The idea appealed to Stewart, and soon she was applying for stock market jobs. After a few failures, she interviewed at a young, fast-growing firm run by Andrew J. Monness. Monness took one look at Stewart and saw "instant success." Stewart could impress clients with her good looks, her education, and her knowledge of art and culture. But Monness saw something else. Stewart, he reflected, was from a modest background. Unlike some other Wall Street workers, Stewart was not a "trust-fund baby"—someone born into wealth and privilege. If trust-fund babies grew bored or unhappy with their jobs, they could just quit. But someone like Stewart knew how to work hard. Monness hired her.

WALL STREET

Stewart began preparing for her new job. She first had to find a nanny to take care of Lexi during the day. Then she had to study for her broker's license. People can only trade on the NYSE if they are trained and licensed. They then become listed as official brokers. Stewart received her license in the fall of 1967.

Traders work the busy floor of the New York Stock Exchange.

The NYSE is what is known as an open outcry auction market. Monday through Fridays, the exchange bell rings at nine o'clock in the morning and trading begins. Down on the exchange floor, brokers wear smocks in their company colors. They cluster around stock posts, places where particular shares are being sold. Workers called specialists run auction-type sales of the shares. Brokers shout out to the specialists how many shares they want to buy or sell. Millions of shares are exchanged this way every day on the NYSE floor. Brokers are paid by fees or on commission (a portion of the purchase price) for each exchange. It is a loud, fast-paced, and aggressive environment.

THE STOCK MARKET

I n the United States, *stock* refers to shares of owner-ship in a company. If a company is publicly traded on the stock exchange, members of the public can buy shares in the company. Most often they buy these shares through a stockbroker. The more shares peo-ple own in a company, the more power they have to influence company business decisions. But company leaders are required by law to run the business in the best interests of all its stock-holders. After all, people buy shares and own stock in order to make money.

Stockbrokers protect their clients by monitoring the ups and downs of the stock market. If shares in a company begin to fall in value, a stockbroker might advise his or her client to sell the shares. If values begin to rise, the broker might tell the client to buy more. Stockbrokers also analyze the market for trends and make predictions about which stocks will become "hot" (rapidly rising in value). Brokers can then advise their clients to buy those up-and-coming stocks while they are still cheap.

When Stewart began as a stockbroker, very few women worked in stock exchanges. No rules prohib-ited women from having a broker's license. But it was not traditionally a field for women. Stewart, however, found that her drive and ambition were a good fit for the NYSE. "We worked very hard," she said. "We started every day at zero. I learned how to be really competitive there." Despite the pressure, Stewart liked her job. Her clients were interesting, wealthy men, and she enjoyed going out to business dinners with them at the best restaurants in New York. She also enjoyed the money. From 1968 to 1971, Stewart made more than one hundred thousand dollars a year.

TURKEY HILL

While Stewart worked on Wall Street, Andy worked as a corporate lawyer. Both had demanding jobs, but they still had ambitious plans outside the office. After selling their Middlefield schoolhouse, the couple began looking for another old house to renovate. After the renovation, they planned to resell the house for a profit. But they wanted to be able to live in the house while they remodeled it. Suburban Connecticut seemed a good choice. It was an easy trip into New York City on commuter trains.

Westport, Connecticut, is an old New England town dating back to colonial days. It appeals to many transplanted New Yorkers. It is a wealthy area with boutiques, galleries, fine restaurants, community theaters, and an art center. Residents include movie star couple Paul Newman and Joanne Woodward and writer Erica Jong. The Stewarts believed it would be easy to resell any renovated property there. The problem was finding one they could afford.

While driving through town with a real estate agent, the Stewarts noticed an old, abandoned farmhouse on

Turkey Hill Road. Originally built in 1805, it was a historic structure. But its last owner was an elderly woman who could not keep up with home repairs. After her death, the property was completely neglected. Locals called the house the Westport horror.

The Stewarts checked the property. The house's plumbing and electricity had not been updated in decades. There was no central heating, and the roof leaked. The staircase was dangerous, and the floors were cracked and uneven. The yard was filled with weeds and rusted junk. But it was priced at thirty-four thousand, as cheap a property as the Stewarts would find in Westport. They bought it.

FINDING A CALLING

The couple moved into the house in 1973. With a loan from Andy's company, they began renovations. Every available night after work and on weekends, Stewart and Andy worked on the house's most pressing repairs, such as conforming the electrical wiring to safety codes. But both still put in long hours at their jobs. Stewart often had to dine with clients after business hours and sometimes did not get home until eleven at night. Soon, Stewart and Andy were both nearing exhaustion.

Within months the Stewarts knew they had to make a change. The stock market was in a recession, or temporary decline. Stewart was not making the money she once had. But Andy was making more money than ever. The couple decided that Stewart would stay home full-time. They would not have to worry about finding day care for Lexi, and Stewart could take over much of the renovation. Andy would still help on weekends.

For two years, the Stewarts worked on the house. Family and friends thought they were crazy, but the couple enjoyed it. They tore down interiors walls and tore up flooring. They added bathrooms and installed new kitchen cabinets. The house had seven fireplaces, and the Stewarts repaired each one. Stewart herself directed the construction of a restaurant-sized kitchen.

Outside, the couple renovated the barn and made plans for extensive gardens. The house sat on two acres of land, and the Stewarts purchased a few more acres of adjoining property. They put in an orchard of apple, sour cherry, white peach, pear, and plum trees. In another plot, they planted vegetables, herbs, currants, and blueberries. In her flower garden, Stewart planted all the old-fashioned blooms she loved—roses, snapdragons, irises, and begonias. The Stewarts named the property and house Turkey Hill Farm.

The Stewarts also wanted to raise animals. The property grew to include two beehives housing eighty thousand bees, a second barn, and a henhouse. Turkeys, chickens, and geese roamed the farmyard. Goats and one black sheep occupied the main barn. Stewart encouraged Lexi to take good care of the animals. It became Lexi's special job to bottle feed milk

Stewart and Andy pose outside their Turkey Hill farmhouse in Westport, Connecticut.

to the baby goats. Stewart believed the responsibility would teach the little girl a love of living things.

Inside the roomy house, nine adopted cats and two chow chows—large, furry dogs—shared the Stewarts' space. Every Saturday, Stewart groomed all the pets, giving them baths when needed.

Keeping house, taking care of a child, and cooking meals is a full-time job for many people. But Stewart also tended to the gardens and the orchard. She took care of the animals and worked on home repair and decorating. She often invited family and friends from New Jersey and New York to come for long weekend visits. Her energy seemed endless. She loved her life in Westport. She realized, she said, "that making a home, raising a family, was more important to me than anything else."

THE UNCATERED AFFAIR

In the early 1970s, Stewart was still working through Julia Child's massive cookbook. She had never taken a formal cooking class, but she had been comfortable in a kitchen since childhood. She found it easy to follow recipes and had enough natural talent to make up her own variations. She became well known among her Westport friends as an excellent cook.

Her parents had given her her first cookbook when she was eight. Stewart wanted to pass on those same skills to Lexi. She began giving cooking lessons in her kitchen to Lexi and her young grade-school friends. The children got white chef's hats when they took a class. Stewart taught them how to make simple dishes such as omelets. Soon, Stewart was conducting classes for grown-up friends too.

Stewart also began to advertise in the *Westport News*, the local newspaper, as a caterer. Caterers prepare and serve foods at special functions. Stewart offered her services for cocktail parties, dinners, weddings, and birthday parties. Her first big job was a wedding reception for three hundred guests. Stewart carefully prepared a menu with unique dishes, such as *oeufs en gelée* (eggs in gelatin). She also constructed a lavish wedding cake with buttercream icing.

But as an inexperienced caterer, Stewart failed to take certain factors into account. For example, the reception was being held outdoors in August. On the wedding day, afternoon temperatures neared one hundred degrees. The gelatin melted around the eggs. The cake frosting also began to melt, sending the layers sliding in different directions. Stewart and her assistants managed to save the dishes, repairing them so no guests even noticed. The reception was a success. But Stewart learned an important catering rule: be realistic about your menus.

The reception and all the business that followed also made Stewart realize that she needed a partner. Stewart turned to one of her friends in Connecticut, Norma Collier. The women had known each other since their New York modeling days. They shared many interests— in antiques, crafts, and cooking. Both women saw a real business opportunity in creating gourmet food for the area's busy, upper-middle-class families.

In 1974 they came up with a plan to begin a local catering service. Before a client's party, Collier and Stewart would arrive with most of the food already cooked. They would arrange the food on the client's own serving dishes and leave before the guests arrived. Collier and Stewart called their new business the Uncatered Affair, because the fancy food was served as if their clients had prepared it themselves.

Word-of-mouth recommendations for the Uncatered Affair brought in new business every week. But the partnership between Stewart and Collier quickly soured. Collier complained that Stewart criticized and insulted her in front of clients. She also discovered that Stewart had booked catering jobs without telling her. Stewart intended to work the jobs herself and keep all the profits. The partnership ended in 1975, only months after it began. This was perhaps the first indication that Martha Stewart worked better when she worked alone—or at least when she was completely in charge.

MARTHA IN CHARGE

Despite the setback, Stewart was intent on feeding Westport's appetite for gourmet cooking. In 1976 she rented a small space from some Westport businesses. They were grouped together in a small downtown mall called the Common Market. She set up a sales table and began selling pies, cakes, and cookies to Common Market shoppers. She called her business the Market Basket. Sales were good, despite the high prices of the baked goods. Soon, Stewart moved into her own shop and installed a professional oven and refrigerator. But even with her new equipment, Stewart could not keep up with the demand.

Stewart began organizing local women to supply baked goods and other fresh food for the shop. This arrangement, however, caused Stewart problems with the Westport Health District. There are laws about selling food in commercial establishments. Health inspectors have to check kitchens and food preparation areas to make sure they are sanitary. None of the kitchens of Stewart's Market Basket bakers had been inspected. Health district agents told Stewart that her business would have to get its baked goods from a single, inspected location.

Stewart complied with the health district's rules. But she was already outgrowing the Market Basket. She hired a college student, Vicki Negrin, to operate the shop. Freed from the daily work of running the store, Stewart wrote articles for *Family Circle* magazine and the *New York Times*. She also began a regular column called "Quick Cook" in *House Beautiful* magazine. Stewart continued her catering business, running it from Turkey Hill Farm. She catered events for some of Westport's elite, including Newman and Woodward, actor Robert Redford, and opera singer Beverly Sills. By 1977 she had decided to consolidate, or bring all her business efforts together. Stewart's businesses had become successful because of the delicious food, beautiful table presentations, and reliable operations. But Stewart had also been skillful enough to keep her image in the foreground. She sold herself as the creative mind behind the chocolate tarts and the floral centerpieces. When she consolidated her businesses, she knew that she was famous enough to trade on her name. So she called her new operation Martha Stewart, Inc.

MARTHA INCORPORATED

In her early days at Turkey Hill Farm, Stewart said she enjoyed nothing better than taking care of her home and family. But as her success as a caterer grew, she seemed thrilled by the money, the praise, and the chance to mingle with the rich and famous. Her work often kept her away from her family. Lexi sometimes helped out at catering jobs, but as she got older, she was away at boarding school in Vermont. Andy supported Stewart's business by recommending Martha Stewart, Inc., to clients. But on a day-to-day basis, much of his time and energy went into his own demanding job. Despite these family pressures, Stewart seemed intent on growing her business.

She converted the basement of the Turkey Hill Farm house into a catering kitchen. She installed the professional equipment she had bought for the Market Basket. Here, she cooked all the food for catered events, tested new recipes, and offered cooking classes.

As Stewart's business grew, some private problems began to surface. In the spring of 1977, Andy was diagnosed with cancer. The family was shocked by the news. Andy then endured months of treatments and eventually beat the disease. But his deadly battle did not seem to unite the couple. In fact, friends noticed that the Stewarts' relationship was failing.

Stewart prepares dough in her large, well-stocked kitchen.

In their early days in New York, friends recalled, the couple always seemed very happy. But as Stewart grew busier and more successful, she seemed to lose patience with her quiet, unassuming husband. Weekend guests at Turkey Hill Farm reported that they were embarrassed by Stewart's sarcastic remarks about Andy. It seemed that in Stewart's eyes, Andy was not making enough money and not doing enough around the house. And if he was doing something, he was doing it wrong. One of Stewart's stockbroker friends, Sandy Greene, recalls, "On Wall Street she had a healthy competitiveness, but eventually it turned nasty. She became very demanding."

Some Stewart critics have also wondered where Lexi fit into the Stewarts' life. Stewart had said that she loved Turkey Hill Farm because it reminded her how important family life was. But as Lexi entered junior high school, both parents seemed to be spending most of their time on their careers. Lexi was enrolled in an expensive Connecticut day school and given dance lessons. But she is hardly mentioned in accounts of the Stewarts' Westport life. Was Stewart just protecting the privacy of her shy, young daughter? Or was Lexi pushed to the background of her parents' busy lives?

In 1979 the Stewarts suffered another emotional blow. Edward Kostyra died following a heart attack. That left Stewart to sort out her feelings for her father. "[He] was not so satisfied with his lot in life," Stewart said, "and I've tried to figure that out." She did not understand why her father, with six bright kids and a loving wife, had been unhappy. Instead, he had often been demanding and angry. Yet Stewart knew that he, more than anyone else, had encouraged and taught her.

Whatever emotions the Stewarts struggled with, they did not slow down their careers. By the late 1970s, Andy had switched from corporate law to publishing, taking a job with the Times Mirror Company. He was put in charge of the Harry Abrams imprint (the name under which a publisher issues books). That part of the company was known for art books and other illustrated publications. One of the projects Andy contracted for

Andy is surrounded by gnomes in his Henry Abrams office during the publication of the hit book Gnomes.

Abrams was a picture book about gnomes, little forest creatures from Germanic legend. *Gnomes* became an overnight sensation. The book spawned a gnome craze. Posters, calendars, clocks, and Christmas ornaments featured the tiny beings with pointy hats.

Andy followed the success of *Gnomes* with a similar book called *Fairies*. He asked Stewart to cater a publishing party for *Fairies* in New York City. At the party, Andy overheard a guest exclaim how delicious the food was. Andy explained that his wife was the caterer. The guest turned out to be Alan Merkin, the head of Crown Publishing. Andy introduced the two, and Merkin asked Stewart if she would be interested in writing a cookbook. Within weeks Andy had negotiated a deal between Stewart and Crown's Clarkson Potter imprint.

Stewart was an untried, first-time author, but she made a few things clear to her Clarkson Potter editors. She knew exactly how she wanted her book to be done. She wanted it to be full of color photographs, even though many cookbooks at the time had only black-and-white photos. She wanted to include not only recipes but advice, stories, and instruction on the entire topic of home entertaining. In fact, that is what she wanted to call the book: *Entertaining*.

Her editors decided to let Stewart follow her instincts, and she began work on the project. In 1981 she converted one of the Turkey Hill Farm buildings into a kitchen and offices and moved Martha Stewart, Inc. there. She used the kitchen to test all the recipes for *Entertaining*. Meanwhile, Michael Shott took photographs of Turkey Hill Farm and of Stewart working. Writer Elizabeth Hawes helped Stewart shape the book's stories and instructions. And Andy sorted though all the photos, picking out the best. He also did much of the book's page layout—deciding how to fit recipes, text, and photos on a page.

Stewart continued her catering business while working on the book. The catering expanded into Manhattan and into more lavish events. She hired three assistant cooks.

For her waitstaff, she hired high school and college students and young New York actors. She catered parties in Manhattan landmarks such as the Metropolitan Museum of Art, the U.S. Customs House (a former government building), and Lincoln Center (a complex for opera, dance, and other performing arts). For a cocktail party held by the Museum of American Folk Art, Stewart and her staff served fifteen hundred guests in a vast, unused building on a Manhattan wharf. The place had no decorations or even a kitchen. Stewart had to plan for, buy, cook, and truck in everything.

Stewart, right, *and friend Ruth Leserman prepare dishes for a luncheon to celebrate the publication of* Entertaining.

ENTERTAINING

Entertaining was published in 1982. At thirty-five dollars, it was one of the most expensive cookbooks on the market. But despite the high price, its first printing of twenty-five thousand copies sold out quickly. *Entertaining* became a best seller. Stewart had found a ready audience for her ideas on stylish parties and carefully prepared foods.

By the time the book arrived in stores, the decade of the 1980s was already shaping up as a period of "conspicuous consumption." Conspicuous consumption refers to the practice of buying things as symbols of social and economic status, rather than for practical reasons. Luxury cars, exotic vacations, designer clothing, and gourmet food and wine are ways to show off wealth.

Another popular trend was Anglophilia, or the love of English culture. About one billion television viewers around the world had watched Britain's Prince Charles marry Lady Diana Spencer in London in 1981. The event sparked U.S. interest in the British aristocracy, or nobility. Magazines, movies, and the television miniseries *Brideshead Revisited* further popularized British aristocratic life. Many people in the United States began to take great interest in the traditions and styles found in British country homes.

Stewart had decorated Turkey Hill Farm in a very traditional style. Her carefully collected antiques, silver tableware, china, and table linens were all on display in *Entertaining*. This aspect of the book appealed to many American readers who wanted to bring a touch of aristocratic elegance to their suburban homes.

At the beginning of *Entertaining*, Stewart explains that parties and dinners are no longer bound by "severe and detailed instructions for the handling of social habits and rituals." Dinner does not have to be served at precisely six thirty. Ladies do not have to wear gloves and hats to visit neighbors. People entertain, Stewart writes, because they want to celebrate.

Stewart also believed in the importance of using individual style and in making guests feel at ease. "I think it's very, very important to use your own individuality. You can express yourself creatively and still just be a regular person." But it could be said that much of *Entertaining*'s appeal lay in its formality and tradition—the beautifully set tables and carefully prepared food. People wanted to project style and ease, but they wanted to make sure they were doing it correctly. For many suburban-raised, middle-class baby boomers, *Entertaining* answered a lot of questions.

Some Stewart critics have suggested that *Entertaining* may also have appealed to middle-class people because it presented the home as a refuge. In the 1980s, most families had two working parents. Weekdays could be long and stressful. Stewart presented a vision of the family house as a peaceful place of delicious dinners and beautiful but comfortable rooms.

Not everyone, however, loved *Entertaining*. Some feminists—people who support women's equal rights—

scoffed at Stewart's old-fashioned approach to home-making. What wife or mother, they asked, is going to bake bread or make mayonnaise from scratch when she has to work all day? Other critics claimed that the recipes were not workable—that they contained incorrect measurements or faulty instructions.

A few critics even claimed that some of the recipes were plagiarized, or taken from other published sources without permission. Stewart dismissed accusations that she plagiarized on purpose. She claimed that she had been collecting and adapting recipes for years from many places and had not taken exact recipes from other books. But author Barbara Tropp proved that *Entertaining* included several recipes from her book, *The Modern Art of Chinese Cooking*. Tropp and Stewart reportedly resolved the matter without going to court.

But bad reviews and legal claims failed to slow down the sales of *Entertaining*. Stewart's fans far outnumbered her critics, and her newborn publishing career thrived.

In the 1980s, Stewart became a symbol of culinary success. Here, she taste tests a slice of cake at The National Pastry Competition's Let Them Eat Cake event in New York City.

Chapter **FOUR**

A MEDIA
EMPIRE

FOLLOWING THE SUCCESS OF *ENTERTAINING,* STEWART
published more books. In 1983 *Martha Stewart's Quick
Cook* came out. It featured meals that could, Stewart
claimed, be prepared in less than one hour. She followed that with *Martha Stewart's Hors d'Oeuvres*
(1984), a book on finger foods and appetizers, and
Martha Stewart's Pies and Tarts (1985).

She continued her catering business and still wrote
newspaper and magazine columns. But to this already
busy schedule she added book tours, lectures, and
speaking engagements at charity events. At her Westport
headquarters, Stewart also began to offer seminars on
entertaining. Fans paid nine hundred to twelve hundred
dollars to attend the three- or four-day seminars on

Stewart shows off a table full of decorations to a group of women attending one of her entertaining seminars.

cooking and serving gourmet foods. Stewart employees and sometimes Stewart herself gave seminar guests tours of Turkey Hill Farm and the Stewart home.

In 1986 Stewart hosted her first television special on the Public Broadcasting System (PBS). *Holiday Entertaining* featured Stewart giving advice on winter holiday dinners and parties. As the show's centerpiece, she created a turkey baked in a pastry crust, decorated with cutout pastry leaves. She also provided a video tour of the Stewart house at Turkey Hill Farm, which again provided fans with an example of the perfect home for entertaining. She followed the PBS special with a set of how-to videotapes. She also began working with Hawes on *Weddings*, a book for brides, grooms, and their families.

MIXED REVIEWS

Just ten years after she began the Market Basket, Stewart's catering and publishing business was a $1 million enterprise. Her books and TV programs appealed to men and women alike. Actor Dennis Franz, known for playing the tough police officer Andy Sipowicz on *NYPD Blue*, admits to being a Stewart fan. Franz says he and his wife, Joanie, particularly like Stewart's ability to set a beautiful table.

But despite having loyal fans, Stewart also became an object of mocking criticism. Her vocal critics claimed that her projects and recipes were ridiculously time consuming and unrealistic. "They're so overdone, so complicated," laughed Diane White, a writer for the *Boston Globe* newspaper. The pastry-covered turkey dinner from the PBS special, for example, had actually taken ten people four days to prepare.

Some Stewart fans countered the mocking by claiming that Stewart's loudest critics are East Coast media people not interested in cooking or home crafts anyway. Other fans explained that they had no intention of completely re-creating the Martha Stewart lifestyle. They just liked to read the beautifully illustrated books and pick and choose among the recipes and projects.

Another common charge leveled against Stewart at this time was that she appealed mostly to WASPs—white, Anglo-Saxon Protestants. People of color and people with strong ethnic backgrounds were not part of the world glimpsed on the pages of *Entertaining*. Stewart herself, critics said, had downplayed her Polish working-class background. She had gotten rid of her New Jersey accent and re-created herself as the perfect blonde Connecticut socialite.

Perhaps in part to answer this charge of elitism, Stewart made a surprising business decision in 1987. She became a spokesperson for Kmart, a discount retail chain known for its "blue-light specials" (in-store sales) and its cheaply made clothes and house-wares. Kmart signed Stewart to a $5 million, five-year

Stewart examines the packaging of one of her household accessories at Kmart.

contract. According to the Stewart agreement, Stewart would introduce a line of paint colors, bed linens, and bath towels to be sold exclusively at Kmart stores. Kmart thus had a chance to spruce up its image, while Stewart had the opportunity to reach a whole new market of fans.

A MARRIAGE ENDS

Weddings hit the bookshelves in 1987, and forty-six-year-old Stewart set off on a promotional tour. Weddings had become big business during the early 1980s. Brides and their families spent huge amounts of money on dresses, food, and decorations. Newly engaged women were eager for Martha Stewart's advice on creating the perfect, romantic wedding day. The book was a success. Throughout the *Weddings* tour, fans waited for hours to talk to Stewart and to ask her to sign their copies of the book.

But while Stewart toured the country dispensing wedding advice, her own marriage fell apart. In the summer of 1987, Andy moved out of the Turkey Hill Farm house. He claimed that he was tired of the endless work involved in Martha Stewart, Inc. He just wanted to live his own life. Stewart tried to keep her personal life out of the spotlight as she completed the *Weddings* tour. But the press leaped at the news that the perfect U.S. housewife had been dumped by her husband. Fans, however, rallied around Stewart. Stewart observers remark that the trauma may have made Stewart seem more human and vulnerable.

After Andy left, news surfaced that he was having an extramarital affair with one of Stewart's assistants, Robyn Fairclough. Friends reported that tension had grown almost unbearable between Stewart and Andy in the months before the split. But Stewart was apparently completely unaware of the affair. According to some reports in the tabloid press (newspapers that strongly feature gossip), she reacted very badly. Tabloids claimed that Stewart followed Fairclough in her car, screaming insults at her.

The Stewarts' divorce file also reportedly contained a complaint that Stewart had "created a scene" at Andy's Manhattan office. Stewart, Andy claimed, had shown up during business hours and tried to break a window. Andy also claimed that Stewart had sent harassing and insulting letters to Fairclough and her parents. As a result, Andy obtained a restraining order, a court decree forbidding Stewart to contact him. Andy and Stewart were only allowed to speak to each other through their lawyers. They were barred from entering each other's homes and offices.

During their separation, Andy and Stewart also battled over money. Andy felt that he had helped Stewart build her empire and was entitled to part of it. Stewart argued that Andy had walked out on the marriage and had humiliated her in public. The couple also fought for Lexi's loyalty. Both parents had neglected

Lexi in favor of their careers. But during the divorce, both worried about losing contact with her permanently. Eventually, during the two-year divorce proceedings, the Stewarts worked out their money issues. Lexi, by then a Barnard College graduate and independent adult, had to forge new relationships with both her parents.

After her marriage ended, Stewart had trouble sleeping. Her sister Laura and old friends such as Kathy Tatlock noticed that Stewart neglected her appearance, even when she was scheduled for interviews and video shoots. She seemed sad and, for someone with boundless energy, very weary. Marriage had been important to Stewart, her friend Mariana Pasternak explained. Even though she had neglected her relationship with Andy, Stewart had never imagined not being married to him. Left alone at Turkey Hill Farm, Stewart tried to readjust. Pasternak said, "It took her quite a long time to redesign that world for herself." Stewart herself admitted that she understood that Andy had tired of her ambitions and her growing business. She said, "If I should be punished for being too critical or too perfectionist, I've been punished."

MARTHA STEWART LIVING

Her divorce from Andy was a personal low for Stewart. She had lost her husband of twenty-seven years. "I thought this was all my fault for a long time," she said later. "How could I let everything fall apart like this?" Stewart credits her work with helping her recover from the emotional loss.

She began looking for another home, hoping it would represent a new start. She kept Turkey Hill Farm, inviting her widowed mother to live there. For herself, she purchased a Manhattan apartment on Fifth Avenue overlooking Central Park. She also bought a $1.6 million house in East Hampton, New York. East Hampton is a fashionable town on Long Island, not far from New York City. Stewart's new East Hampton neighbors included singer Billy Joel and fashion designer Calvin Klein.

Stewart poured her returning energy into her business. She had succeeded at books, newspapers, radio,

Stewart's East Hampton home is located on Lilly Pond Road.

and videos. A logical next step was to create a magazine. She imagined the magazine as the essence of Martha Stewart, Inc. Every issue would be filled with recipes, decorating tips, craft ideas, and gardening advice. She presented the magazine idea to several New York media companies, but none was interested. Specialized magazines are a publishing risk. They are expensive to make, and their appeal is often too limited to pay off. In addition, the stock market and the U.S. economy had taken a downturn from the money-making days of the early 1980s. The late 1980s slid into a period of economic recession. Publishers doubted that people were going to spend several dollars on a glossy magazine about mixing and matching china patterns and repotting begonias.

Finally, in 1991, Stewart got media giant Time Warner to take an interest. They agreed to give *Martha Stewart Living* a limited trial run. They would publish 250,000 copies of *Living* and see how it sold. The magazine, as the saying goes, flew off the shelves. It was one of the most profitable starts in magazine history.

In 1993 Stewart began a syndicated (sold to several companies at the same time) television show based on the magazine. The TV show *Martha Stewart Living* provided Stewart with an hour to do as she pleased. Some episodes focused on cooking, with Stewart making a recipe with the help of a New York chef, her mother, or even a few children. In other episodes, she demonstrated a how-to craft or a decorating or gardening project. Stewart won a daytime TV award for Outstanding Service Show Host for the 1994–1995 season.

Television also conferred on Stewart a rare status among celebrities—being known by her first name only. "That's so Martha" became a catchphrase for a carefully decorated cake, formal table setting, or elaborate floral arrangement.

MARTHA THE CONTROL FREAK

Stewart's power as a businesswoman could not be underestimated. But the tabloid press—and often the mainstream press—still found plenty to write about in Stewart's private life. Her 1995 purchase of a second home in East Hampton brought her into conflict with her neighbor, Harry Macklowe. Stewart and Macklowe began a running argument over landscaping plans for the border of their properties. The neighbors fought most of their battles in court. But in May 1997, the conflict took a new and somewhat outrageous twist.

Matthew Munnich was a young landscaper working for Macklowe. One night around nine o'clock, Munnich was packing up equipment when a dark SUV pulled into Macklowe's driveway. According to a complaint filed by Munnich with the local police, the driver, a blonde woman, began swearing at him. She accused him of installing a fence along the property boundary.

Munnich realized that the driver was Macklowe's neighbor, Martha Stewart. Munnich protested that he had nothing to do with any fence. When she would not listen, he began to walk away. According to Munnich, Stewart then tried to back out of the driveway. Munnich found himself caught between the SUV and a cement security box. He yelled at Stewart to stop. In the disputed version of events, Munnich claims that Stewart then turned, looked right at him, and kept backing up. Munnich was forced to dive into some bushes to avoid getting run over. Stewart's companions, Munnich claims, laughed as they drove off.

The local district attorney (the county or state lawyer who brings cases to court) chose not to press criminal charges against Stewart. The press nevertheless had a field day. The story of millionaire neighbors bickering with each other over a fence was surprising enough. But the image of Stewart trying to run over a hapless gardener with her luxury SUV was shocking. The event seemed to confirm the growing collection of rumors passed to the media by neighbors, friends of Andy, and ex-employees. Stewart was rude and arrogant. She was verbally abusive. She was a ruthless control freak.

Stewart often did little to counter the stories. Perhaps she thought they were too ridiculous. Or perhaps, as she grew more powerful, she was less interested in wearing a velvet glove over her iron fist.

When she dealt with clients as a stockbroker or a caterer, she had to please them and give them what they wanted. But as the head of her own company, she expected people to please her and follow her direction.

"I have to be the hard-nosed negotiator," she said. Her most important duty was to protect and grow the business she had created. And she did. By 1995 *Entertaining* had sold almost one million copies. She had published thirteen books in all. *Martha Stewart Living* magazine had a circulation of more than one million. The television show was broad-

Among Stewart's many published books are What to Have for Dinner, *left, and* Desserts, *right.* Stewart personally appears on the covers of most of her books.

cast daily on 177 stations across the United States. Whatever Stewart was doing seemed to be working.

THE EMPIRE GROWS

In 1997 Kmart offered Stewart a $500 million contract to continue their business relationship. With this money, Stewart decided to form Martha Stewart Living Omnimedia. She bought her magazine from Time Warner and launched a website. Marthastewart.com offered recipes, crafts projects, and gardening advice, just as the magazine and show did. It also featured a section where fans could buy household products and cooking equipment.

In 1999 MSLO was listed on the NYSE, an action known as going public. Until then, MSLO had been a privately owned company. But once it was listed on the NYSE, it became a publicly traded company. Members of the public could buy shares in the company.

The day MSLO went public, a huge brightly colored banner outside the NYSE announced the event. As news cameras flashed, Stewart rang the opening bell on the floor of the stock exchange. Then, in a touch that was "so Martha," she helped serve freshly squeezed orange juice and brioche (a French pastry bread) to NYSE employees and stockbrokers.

At the time of its listing, MSLO had been valued at $1.7 billion dollars. Stewart was one of the

Stewart rings the opening bell at the New York Stock Exchange in 1999 to celebrate MSLO going public. Pictured with her are NYSE president William Johnson, left, and MSLO president and chief operating officer Sharon Patrick, right.

wealthiest self-made businesswomen in history. As a public company, MSLO had a board of directors to report on the business to its stockholders. But as chairperson of the board, Stewart still played the biggest part in operations. Money coming in from stockholders would allow Stewart to consider expanding into other areas. One plan she considered was a chain of Martha Stewart stores in malls across the United States. But most important to Stewart—and to her legion of fans—was that she would remain the creative force behind the empire.

Stewart poses on the set of her television show.

Chapter **FIVE**

DOWNFALL

IN THE YEARS FOLLOWING **MSLO'S** STOCK MARKET debut (first appearance), the company became a mainstay for cooks and home decorating fans across the country. Stewart's recipes were widely varied. Her craft projects were inventive. And the products she sold on her website were high quality and affordable. Visitors to the website could buy fresh flowers and even CDs of Stewart's favorite music. Stewart and her company seemed unstoppable.

Then, in June 2002, news broke that Stewart was under investigation for illegal insider trading. Some insider trading is legal if it is properly reported. Illegal insider trading refers to the buying and selling of stock based on important information not available to the public. It is considered a form of fraud, or deliberate deception, because it gives certain stockholders an unfair advantage over other stockholders. The U.S. Department of Justice (DOJ) and the Securities and Exchange Commission (SEC) were both investigating Stewart for securities fraud, (illegal investing or trading of stock). The DOJ investigates federal crimes (such as securities fraud). The SEC is a federal agency that, among other things, monitors sales and practices among stock market traders.

The Stewart investigation stemmed from an incident six months earlier. On December 27, 2001, Stewart had quickly sold off her shares in a company just before its NYSE value dropped. That raised a red flag with the SEC that Stewart had information about the stock collapse in advance. Investigators believed such advance information, unavailable to the public, would have to have come from an executive inside the company.

The stock in question was in ImClone Systems, Inc., a biotechnology firm that researches new medical treatments and processes. ImClone had developed a drug, Erbitux, which seemed to have strong potential for treating colon cancer. ImClone's stock prices had risen on the positive "buzz" over Erbitux. But in 2001, the U.S. Food and Drug Administration (FDA) was still testing Erbitux to make sure it was safe to give to cancer patients. The drug's success—and much of ImClone's finances—rested on the FDA's final decision.

By December 2001, rumors swirled around Wall Street that the FDA was not happy with the tests on Erbitux.

WHO DID WHAT AND WHEN?

On December 24, the FDA called ImClone's founder and chief executive, Samuel Waksal. It would not be approving Erbitux. Waksal knew what that meant. ImClone's stock prices had already been sliding due to recent Wall Street rumors. When news of the final FDA decision became public, ImClone stocks would be almost worthless. Waksal and his family had much of their personal fortunes tied up in tens of thousands of ImClone shares. They would be financially ruined. Waksal, on vacation in the Caribbean Islands, immediately flew back home to New York.

ImClone founder Sam Waksal speaks with reporters after leaving court in 2002.

THE SUMMER OF SCANDALS

long period of corporate scandals in the United States began in the fall of 2001. In October news broke that the DOJ and the SEC were investigating Enron, an energy company. Investigators accused Enron executives of fraud, such as hiding debts, forming illegal partnerships, and bribing foreign governments. Enron's accounting firm, Arthur Anderson, came under fire too. The firm was found to have shredded documents that proved Enron's guilt.

CEO Jeff Skilling was one of the Enron executives convicted of fraud.

Enron's widely publicized downfall was followed by other corporate disasters. By March 2002, WorldCom (a telecommunications company) was under investigation for cheating investors out of billions of dollars. In April 2002, the owners of Adelphi Communications were accused of using company money to give themselves $3 billion worth of illegal loans. In July 2002, AOL Time Warner, the world's largest media company, was investigated for inflating profits to make the company look better.

Executives at Bristol-Meyer Squibb (a drug firm), Tyco (a large manufacturing corporation), Halliburton (an oil and gas supplier), and ten other corporations also came under investigation between May and August 2002. The media began calling this the summer of scandals.

Once in New York, Waksal called his investment firm, Merrill Lynch. He wanted to talk to his stockbroker, Peter Bacanovic. According to federal investigators, Waksal wanted his daughter and his father to sell all their shares in ImClone as soon as the market opened on December 26. Waksal also allegedly tried to have his own shares transferred to his daughter so she could sell them without drawing the attention of the SEC. The Waksal shares were sold as planned.

Bacanovic had also left New York to celebrate the holidays in a warmer climate. He was in Florida. His assistant, Douglas Faneuil, was in the Merrill Lynch office taking all Waksal's calls. When Bacanovic checked with Faneuil on December 27, he got the news that the Waksals had dumped their ImClone stock.

That same day, Bacanovic placed a call to another ImClone stockholder and his most important client—Martha Stewart. Stewart was on her way to Mexico. When her plane stopped in Texas to refuel, Stewart picked up Bacanovic's message from her assistant, Ann Armstrong. Thinking Bacanovic was in New York, Stewart immediately called the Merrill Lynch office. She talked to Faneuil and, that day, sold her 3,928 shares in ImClone.

Investigators discovered that another phone call had taken place on December 27. Stewart had tried to call Sam Waksal. Stewart and Waksal shared more than a Merrill Lynch stockbroker. They were, in fact, old friends and were due to meet in Mexico for New Year's Eve. Stewart did not get through to Waksal. Instead, she left a message asking, in effect, "What's going on with ImClone?"

The investigation into Stewart's stock sale rested on this pattern of phone calls. To sum it up: Waksal called Bacanovic, Bacanovic called Stewart, Stewart called Waksal, and Stewart and Waksal dumped their ImClone stock within a day of each other. These facts did not look like innocent coincidences to federal investigators.

The case against Sam Waksal seemed clear-cut. He had obviously tried to dump his family's stock in ImClone based on insider information. But to charge Stewart and Bacanovic with insider trading, investigators would have to prove some very specific things. They had to prove that Stewart and Bacanovic received information from an insider, that they knew the insider should not have given them that information, and that they then intentionally committed fraud by trading on that information.

The case against Stewart and Bacanovic did not seem strong. Waksal was the ImClone insider, not Bacanovic or Stewart. If Waksal had provided Stewart with an insider tip, why did she call him and leave a message asking what was going on? For their part, Faneuil and Bacanovic argued that they told Stewart that ImClone prices were dropping, not that Waksal was dumping his stock. And by the time Stewart sold her shares, she was not alone in doing so. On December 26, 1.5 million shares of ImClone stock had been traded on the NYSE. By December 27, that number had shot up to 8 million.

In further defense of their actions, Stewart and Bacanovic told investigators that they had a verbal agreement regarding ImClone stock. Bacanovic claimed that he was never confident in ImClone's future and did not want Stewart to keep the stock. But Stewart, out of loyalty to Waksal, would not sell it. As a compromise, the pair agreed that Bacanovic would automatically sell ImClone stock if the price ever dropped below sixty dollars per share. When Stewart sold her stock on December 27, the shares were valued at fifty-eight dollars.

Normally, a broker and an investor formalize this type of agreement with a document called a stop-loss order. But Stewart and Bacanovic had never filed a stop-loss, so there was no paper trail to prove their agreement. Daniel Faneuil backed up his boss and Stewart. But investigators were suspicious. The verbal agreement seemed too convenient. They put heavy pressure on Faneuil, and in June 2002, he changed his story. There was no verbal agreement, he said, and Bacanovic had asked him to lie to investigators. Furthermore, he said Bacanovic had told Stewart on December 27, 2001, that Waksal had dumped his ImClone stock.

Investigators spent the next year making their case against Stewart and Bacanovic. Despite Faneuil's testimony, investigators still could not prove that Stewart traded on insider information. But on June 4, 2003, Stewart and Bacanovic were indicted, or formally charged, in U.S. district court for obstruction of justice, conspiracy, making false statements, and securities fraud (for lying to investigators). Stewart fans were shocked and dismayed.

But even some people who were not necessarily interested in Stewart wondered about the validity of the charges. Lawyer Michael McMenamin, writing in *Reason Online* (a political journal website) in October 2003, harshly criticized insider trading laws as vague and "murky." Investigators did not have enough direct evidence to charge Stewart for the serious crime of insider trading. So, McMenamin wrote, they charged her with denying that she had received the stock tip. "In other words," he blasts, "her crime is claiming to be innocent of a crime with which she was never charged."

THE FALLOUT

Innocent or not, Stewart's indictment had an effect on her empire even before the trial began. The criminal investigation and the charges cost Stewart an estimated $400 million in legal fees and business losses. As MSLO stock prices dropped, Stewart resigned as chairperson and chief executive officer (CEO) of the company.

The case of the *United States of America v. Martha Stewart and Peter Bacanovic* began in New York on January 28, 2004. In opening statements, both the

Peter Bacanovic, Stewart's stockbroker, leaves the courthouse in March 2004.

defense and the prosecution appealed to the middle-class jury of eight women and four men. Stewart's defense lawyer Robert Morillo portrayed his client as a self-made woman who had risen above her humble New Jersey roots. The prosecution countered by portraying Stewart as a market-savvy millionaire who took advantage of her high-placed social connections to avoid losing even a tiny part of her enormous fortune.

During the course of the trial, Faneuil and Ann Armstrong testified for the prosecution. Faneuil recounted his story about lying for Bacanovic to investigators. Armstrong admitted that Stewart had asked her to erase a phone log entry for December 27, 2001, regarding a call between Stewart and Bacanovic. And Mariana Pasternak, who was with Stewart in Mexico in December 2001, testified that Stewart mentioned getting some kind of insider tip. Stewart did not testify in her own defense.

The case against Stewart and Bacanovic was not overwhelming. But neither was the case *for* them. The jury believed Faneuil, the prosecution's key witness. They also were baffled as to why Stewart did not take the stand to defend herself. "I was ready to hear her side," juror Dana D'Allessandro said. "No matter who they put on, I wanted to hear from her." In the end, the jurors felt that the prosecution had presented the stronger argument.

On March 5, 2004, the verdict was handed down. The judge, Miriam Cedarbaum, dismissed the charge of securities fraud. But both Stewart and Bacanovic were found guilty of obstruction of justice, conspiracy, and making false statements—all felony charges. Lexi, who had attended every day of the trial, broke down in tears as the verdict was read.

After the trial, Stewart gave a press conference. "I will appeal the verdict and continue to fight to clear my name," she said. Some high-profile Stewart defenders also came forward to question the federal government's case. The *Wall Street Journal, Forbes,* and *Business Week,* all influential financial publications, bashed the "scapegoating" of Stewart during a period of corporate scandals. "Prosecutors abused their power to make an example of [Stewart]," Diane Brady wrote in *Business Week*'s March 2004 issue. Stewart's misconduct was personal, Brady argued, not corporate. "Martha Stewart didn't cook the books (keep deliberately inaccurate accounting records). She didn't loot her company. Nor did she set out to dupe her investors."

Questions about the trial lingered, but the damage to MSLO was done. Within a week of her conviction, Stewart resigned from MSLO's board of directors. She also gave up her membership to the New York Stock Exchange. Advertisers began pulling their ads from *Martha Stewart Living,* and CBS canceled Stewart's television show. Stock prices in MSLO dropped dramatically. And the SEC announced plans to pursue civil charges against Stewart—noncriminal charges that could result in monetary fines and business penalties.

In July 2004, Cedarbaum sentenced Stewart to five months in prison, followed by five months' house arrest. Peter Bacanovic received an identical sentence. The sentence was the minimum Cedarbaum could impose under federal guidelines.

Cedarbaum did not immediately announce where or when Stewart should report to prison. And with her appeal still pending, Stewart was free for the time being. She took the opportunity to prepare MSLO for her absence—and her return. Sharon Patrick, a longtime Stewart colleague, took over as CEO. For the position of company director, Stewart hired Charles Koppelman, a wealthy businessperson known for his ability to manage

Stewart is led from the courthouse by U.S. marshals after she was sentenced to five months in prison in July 2004.

publicity crises. Stewart also began planning media events and new ventures to follow her release from prison. Stewart was ready for her comeback; but first she wanted to get prison out of the way.

In September 2004, she asked Cedarbaum to allow her to begin her sentence immediately. Stewart believed delaying her jail time would only continue to hurt the company financially. "Making a decision to stop the bleeding was very important," Stewart said. "I had to stop the bleeding." The judge agreed, and on October 8, 2005, Stewart reported to Alderson Federal Prison Camp.

Behind Bars

According to other Alderson inmates, Stewart spent her first day in prison "walking around in a daze." Prison authorities worried that Stewart might become a target of inmate abuse or violence, so they watched her carefully. In a postprison interview on *Late Night with David Letterman*, Stewart recalled an early incident where she slipped on a wet floor and banged her arm. Prison officials were convinced she had been attacked. "They wanted to know who I had been in a fight with," she said.

In reality, Stewart found that most inmates were friendly, and she settled in to prison life without any incidents. For many women prisoners, the lack of privacy, separation from loved ones, and boredom are difficult adjustments. Stewart certainly missed her freedom and her home. But she was not one to grow bored. "This was the first time in a long time that [Stewart] had time to think about things other than hitting [deadlines]," said her friend Memrie Lewis. Stewart filled her days with yoga classes, reading and writing, Spanish studies, and craft projects.

Stewart was also able to indulge her love of the outdoors and of cooking. Because most Alderson inmates are convicted of nonviolent crimes, they have more freedom than is common in other prisons. Inmates are allowed to wander the prison's one-hundred-acre rural campus. They are only required to check in at four in the afternoon and for the night. Stewart roamed Alderson's fields looking for ways to spruce up the prison's dull cafeteria food. She gathered dandelions, wild greens, and crab apples for salads and desserts. She tried her hand at microwave cooking and even got used to eating from vending machines.

Lexi came to Alderson almost every weekend. She brought Stewart's mother with her as often as possible. Several of Stewart's close friends also visited regularly. But Stewart was quick to realize that she was an exception. Loneliness and poverty were common problems among inmates. "Many of them," she wrote, "have been here for years—devoid of [without any] care, devoid of love, devoid of family." Many of the inmates Stewart met were first-time offenders who had been convicted of nonviolent drug offenses. They were serving long

Lexi, foreground, *supported her mother throughout the ImClone ordeal. Lexi is the majority shareholder in MSLO.*

sentences under harsh federal rules aimed at breaking up serious drug trafficking. Stewart felt that these women would be better off in drug rehabilitation programs. Or, if put in prison, they should be offered education, vocational training, and guidance in coping skills. On her website, she began campaigning against what she saw as unfair federal sentencing guidelines.

Stewart did not forget about outside life while at Alderson. She certainly did not forget about her business. Although she had resigned her top position at the company, she was still a major stockholder. As such, she still wielded power. Watching from prison, Stewart decided that Sharon Patrick was taking the company in the wrong direction. After Stewart's conviction, Patrick had tried to downplay the founder's connection with the company. She felt that Martha Stewart the person (and felon) should be separated from Martha Stewart the brand name. Stewart initially agreed but came to regret the decision. From prison she worked with MSLO officers to replace Patrick with MSLO executive Susan Lyne.

Stewart also continued to prepare for her return by reviewing contracts for postprison television shows. Stewart was not alone in banking on her successful return. During her trial, stock prices in MSLO had dropped from $49 a share to $5.26. The company lost $54 million in six months. But stock prices rose during Stewart's incarceration. Business analysts speculated that Stewart had actually generated sympathy by volunteering to serve her time early. Whatever the motivation, investors registered their belief in a Stewart comeback by snapping up MSLO shares.

Stewart called prison an experience that "has been life altering and life affirming." And most of her descriptions of her time at Alderson reflect those mixed feelings. On one hand, Stewart spoke of fighting depression and called incarceration "pretty horrifying." But on the other hand, she noted "the extraordinary people I have met . . . and all that I have learned." When Stewart left Alderson on March 4, 2005, she took a little bit of the place with her. For the trip home, she wore a handmade poncho given to her by another inmate. And she smuggled out two cuttings from an Alderson ginkgo tree to replant in her home gardens.

Home Again

After Stewart arrived at Cantitoe Farm (purchased in 2000), her estate in Westchester County, New York, she released a brief statement to the press. She was, she said, "thrilled to be returning to my more familiar life." But the life she would lead at Cantitoe, at least for the next few months, was not completely familiar. Stewart was still under house arrest until July 2005.

Under the terms of house arrest, all Stewart's activities had to be approved by her probation officer (the law agent overseeing her release). The probation officer monitored Stewart's whereabouts through the electronic anklet Stewart wore at all times. In some ways, Stewart found house arrest worse than prison. At

Alderson, at least, she was allowed to wander the property. But under house arrest, Stewart could not even step off her front porch at certain times of the day.

Despite the time restrictions and her frequent complaints about how much she hated her anklet, Stewart forged ahead with her typical full schedule. Of her five houses, Stewart had chosen Cantitoe because the property was still under renovation. Knowing it would keep her busy, Stewart set off to turn the estate into "a self-sufficient American farm." She began planting gardens and orchards. She hired a team of Amish (a religious sect that uses only traditional methods of farming and labor) carpenters to build an old-fashioned barn on the property for her farm animals. She oversaw the rehabbing of a separate barn for her five Frisian horses. As always, Stewart took pleasure in the details of running an operation. She watched over the plumbing contractors as they installed sinks in the barns, decided where flowers and trees would be planted, and instructed her grooms to keep her shiny black Frisians out of the sun so their coats would not turn reddish.

THE COMEBACK

While still under house arrest, Stewart was allowed to start working again. During her forty-eight-hour-a-week free time, she traveled to New York City and attended business meetings. She earned $900,000 a year as the founder of MSLO. Company stock was at

Stewart poses with two of her Frisian horses at Cantitoe Farm, shortly after being released from prison in 2005.

an all-time high, and Stewart's share in MSLO was valued at more than $1 billion. The comeback team she had assembled at MSLO welcomed her. Lyne made it clear that her strategy as CEO was to restore Stewart as the public face of MSLO. "It's obvious to anyone looking at the company at this moment," Lyne said, "what huge assets the Martha Stewart brand and Martha Stewart herself are."

Stewart wanted to rehabilitate her image in other media outlets too. She hired high-powered publicist Susan Magrino to handle media appearances. During the stock scandal and trial, Stewart felt that the media deliberately set out to make her look as bad as possible. She relied on Magrino to carefully select interviewers and stage-manage the interviews. She did not mind living in front of a camera, Stewart said, "when it's a friendly camera . . . when I put it there."

In her most famous postprison media deal, Stewart teamed with Hollywood television producer Mark Burnett. Burnett is known as the executive who introduced reality TV to the United States. In 2000 Burnett had started the long-running series *Survivor*. In 2004 Burnett unleashed real estate mogul Donald Trump on prime-time viewers in *The Apprentice*. Burnett wanted Stewart to star in a spin-off of *The Apprentice*. He felt that her comeback would follow "America's favorite storyline"—downfall and redemption.

Stewart did not fit the same management style as the brash and showy Trump. She would not be barking "You're fired" at interns across a boardroom table. "That's Donald," she said. "That's not me." But Stewart arguably has as much business sense as Trump. And Burnett saw other possibilities in her "hidden sense of humor" <5-19> and playful personality. Stewart needed some persuading, but she finally agreed. Allowed to add her own flavor to *The Apprentice: Martha Stewart*, she saw it as a teaching and public relations opening. "It's a wonderful opportunity to show people that I actually have good advice to give to young entrepreneurs, and business lessons to teach."

Burnett and NBC also began plans for a daytime show, *Martha*. This show would focus on cooking and crafts. But unlike the original *Martha Stewart Living*, it would be filmed in front of a live audience. Like *The Apprentice*, it was designed to show Stewart's friendlier, funnier side. Her guests would not be Paris-trained chefs from posh New York restaurants. Rather, they would be popular figures, such as actress Melanie Griffith and soap opera star Deirdre Hall.

Business analysts flooded magazines and newspapers with stories about Stewart's plans. They acknowledged that she needed to make a grand entrance back into the public eye. Her confident return, with the clear support of her company and her fans, would lure advertisers back to *Martha Stewart Living*. The magazine was by far the most successful segment of MSLO, and those advertising dollars were vital. "The real test for Martha will be whether we'll see advertisers really come back," noted analyst Dennis McAlpine. And some observers wondered if her publicity blitz was desperate and unfocused: "[A]ll Martha all the time may prove to be overkill."

Before Stewart could begin her television shows, however, she had to finish her term of house arrest. And in late July 2005, she suffered a setback. She was caught off her property outside her forty-eight-hour free time. Probation officials and Stewart's lawyer, Walter Dellinger, refused to comment on the violation. But the *New York Post* reported that Stewart had been caught going to a yoga class. As punishment, her house arrest was extended by three weeks.

While she served her extended sentence through August 2005, MSLO also suffered a setback. Even as investors bought up shares, the company posted a loss of $33.5 million. It was a much wider loss than the company had suffered while Stewart was in prison. MSLO executives were quick to point out that part of the loss was due to money spent investing in Burnett's television shows. As those shows provided venues for Stewart and all her products, the investment, the company argued, would pay off.

THE NEW MARTHA

Martha debuted on September 12, 2005. *The Apprentice: Martha Stewart* followed on September 21. Both shows generated buzz. But *The Apprentice* drew a relatively small audience. Even given the wide interest in reality TV, only 7 million viewers tuned in. (An average of 21 million viewers watched Trump's first season.) *Martha* did better, but it was also not a blockbuster.

Stewart's personal appearances, on the other hand, were demonstrations of her loyal fan base. In the late fall of 2005, Stewart traveled the United States on a book tour for her new publications, *Martha's Rules* (a business guide) and *Martha Stewart's Baking Handbook*. At bookstores across the country, hundreds of fans lined up in the early hours of the morning, waiting for hours to have their copies signed by Stewart.

THE APPRENTICE: MARTHA STEWART

L ike the original *Apprentice*, Stewart's version featured sixteen contestants trying to win a permanent job at MSLO. Ten women and six men competed to become Stewart's assistant. It meant the chance to learn business know-how from the self-made billionaire.

The contestants ranged in age from twenty-two to forty-two. Among them were advertising executives, lawyers, chefs, and designers. For thirteen weeks, they competed against one another to complete the tasks Stewart assigned. Stewart judged the contestants on their attitude, their sense of organization, and their creativity. Lexi and Charles Koppelman helped her evaluate the candidates.

Martha Stewart: The Apprentice never caught on with TV audiences as Donald Trump's version had. Fans were disappointed by the cancellation, but critics were delighted by the war of words between Stewart and Trump that followed. On the gossip pages of newspapers and *People* magazine, the two billionaires exchanged insults. "It's about

Donald Trump and Stewart confer with each other during a photo shoot for the promotion of both versions of The Apprentice.

time you started taking responsibility for your failed version of *The Apprentice*," Trump scolded Stewart. "Your performance was terrible." Stewart at first expressed shock that her "longtime friend" had said such a thing. But later she fired back: "He's a spoiled brat."

Many fans also welcomed back Stewart's obvious influence on her magazine. Without the "Martha touch," *Martha Stewart Living* had been criticized as bland. It suffered in content and attractiveness next to similar home and lifestyle magazines such as *Real Simple* (published by Time Inc.) and *O* (Oprah Winfrey's magazine). But with Stewart's input, the magazine returned to its unique blend of decorating, housekeeping, and cooking advice. The magazine also grew fatter as advertisers returned. By October 2005, advertising pages in *Martha Stewart Living* had increased by 48 percent over the previous spring.

Stewart's appearance on prime-time television has not been as successful. In December 2005, NBC announced that it would not continue *The Apprentice: Martha Stewart* due to low ratings during its first season. *Martha* has fared a little better, but its format will be adjusted to try to attract more viewers.

THE COMPANY

MSLO's financial situation continues its ups and downs. But says Lyne, "With new initiatives (plans) under way in every area of the business, the revitalization [of MSLO] is firmly underway." Observers say time will tell if that revitalization takes place.

Personally, Stewart is still pursuing her court appeal, hoping to clear her name of the felony charges for which she has already served time. The SEC court case, which is dependent on her appeal, still looms

Martha Stewart Weddings *and* Martha Stewart Living *are displayed on a newsstand in New York City. Both magazines continue to be popular among consumers.*

ahead. If the case is decided against her, Stewart may never be allowed to return to MSLO as an officer or board member.

Financially, Stewart is arguably secure for life. Even if the company fails, she owns a fortune in real estate. But the failure of Martha Stewart Living Omnimedia would mean more than a loss in income. For Martha the Connecticut socialite, MSLO has always been a creative outlet and a business dynamo. For Martha the girl from Nutley, New Jersey, the company has meant security and control. It's something she sacrificed a great deal for—her marriage, friendships, even freedom. The company, she says simply, "is my life's work."

SOURCE NOTES

17 Virginia Meachum, *Martha Stewart: Successful Businesswoman* (Springfield, NJ: Enslow, 1998), 16.
17 *Martha Stewart: It's a Good Thing*, New York: A&E Home Video, 2000.
17 Martha Stewart, interview by Charlie Rose, *Charlie Rose Show*, PBS, July 26, 2005.
18 *Martha Stewart*, A&E video.
18 Stewart, Charlie Rose interview.
18 "Oprah's Cut with Martha Stewart," *O, the Oprah Magazine*, September 2000, http://www.oprah.com/omagazine/200008/omag_200008_martha.jhtml (November 7, 2005).
23 *Martha Stewart*, A&E video.
27 Ibid.
30 "Oprah's Cut with Martha Stewart."
30 *Martha Stewart*, A&E video.
31 Ibid.
38 Ibid.
42 Ibid.
44–45 Stewart, Charlie Rose interview.
49 Ibid.
54 Christopher Byron, *Martha Inc.* (New York: John Wiley and Sons, 2002), 100.
55 Stewart, Charlie Rose interview.
60 Martha Stewart, *Entertaining* (New York: Clarkson Potter, 1982), 12.
60 Stewart, Charlie Rose interview.
65 *Martha Stewart*, A&E video.
68 Byron, 200.
69 *Martha Stewart*, A&E video.
69 Meachum, 42.
69–70 Stewart, Charlie Rose interview.
74 Ibid.
86 Michael McMenamin, "St. Martha," *Reason Online*, October 2003, http://www.reason.com/0310/fe.mm.st.shtml (December 31, 2005).

88 Dave Goldstein, "Where's Martha?" *New York Daily News.com*,
      March 8, 2004, http://www.nydailynews.com/news/
      crime_file/v-pfriendly/story/171479p-149607c.html
      (November 7, 2005).
88 "Martha Stewart," *Hello! Magazine.com*, n.d. http://www
      .hellomagazine.com/profiles/marthastewart (November 7,
      2005).
89 Matt Tyrnauer, "The Prisoner of Bedford," *Vanity Fair*, August
      2005, 178.
90 Ibid.
91 "How Martha Coped at 'Yale'" *CBS News.com*, September 20,
      2005, http://www.cbsnews.com/stories/2005/09/20/
      entertainment/main860422.shtml (September 25, 2005).
91 Ibid.
91 Tyrnauer, 179.
92 Martha Stewart, *Caught in the Net: The Impact of Drug
      Policies on Women and Families*, February 18, 2005,
      http://www.fairlaws4families.com/news/archives/2005/02/
      test.html (November 16, 2005).
94 Krysten Crawford, "Martha, Out and About," *CNN Money.com*,
      March 4, 2005, http://money.cnn.com/2005/
      03/03/news/newsmakers/martha_walkup/index.htm
      (September 25, 2005).
94 "How Martha Coped at 'Yale.'"
94 "Martha Stewart Arrives at N.Y. Home to Begin Detention for
      Lying about Stock Sale," *Court TV.com*, March 4, 2005,
      http://www.courttv.com/trials/stewart/030405_
      ctv.html (September 25, 2005).
94 Crawford.
95 Tyrnauer, 177.
96 Keith Naughton, "Martha Breaks Out," *Newsweek*, March 7,
      2005, 43.
97 David Carr, "Martha Stewart Unchained." *New York Times*,
      August 29, 2005, national edition, C3.
97 Naughton, 41.
97 Tyrnauer, 118.
97 Naughton, 41.
97 Tyrnauer, 118.

98 Shaheen Pasha, "Martha Stewart Unshackled," *CNN Money.com*, August 31, 2005, http://money.cnn.com/2005/ 08/30/news/newsmakers/martha_release/index.htm (September 25, 2005).

98 Ibid.

100 "Trump Skewers Stewart in Open Letter," *People*, February 21, 2006, http://people.aol.com/people/articles/0,19736 ,1161830,00.html (April 2, 2006).

100 "Martha Looks Ready to Bury Hatchet—Right in Donald," *New York Daily News.com*, February 24, 2006, http://www.nydailynews.com/news/gossip/story/ 394202p-334231c.html (April 2, 2006).

101 Anne D'Innocenzio, "Martha Stewart Living's 3Q Loss Widens," *Entertainment News.org*, October 27, 2005, http://www.entertainment-news.org/breaking/37863/ martha-stewart-livings-3q-loss-widens.html (October 29, 2005).

102 "Martha Starts New Life Behind Bars," *CBS News.com*, October 8, 2004, http://www.cbsnews.com/stories/2004/ 09/22/national/main644878.shtml (July 21, 2006).

SELECTED BIBLIOGRAPHY

"About MLO." *Martha Stewart.com*. 2006. http://www
.marthastewart.com/page.jhtml?type=page-cat&id=
cat7&rsc=SC287206 (October 29, 2005).

Buccino, Anthony. *Old Nutley*. Date. http://www.oldnutley.org
(September 18, 2005).

Burns, Greg. "Springing Back After Being Sprung." *Chicago
Tribune*, September 18, 2005. http://www.chicagotribune.com/
business/chi-0509180233sep18 (September 18, 2005).

Byron, Christopher. *Martha Inc.* New York: John Wiley and Sons,
2002.

Carr, David. "Martha Stewart Unchained." *New York Times*,
August 29, 2005, national edition, sec. C.

Crawford, Krysten. "Martha, Out and About." *CNN/Money.com*.
March 4, 2005. http://money.cnn.com/2005/03/03/news/
newsmakers/martha_walkup/index.htm (September 25, 2005).

Goldstein, Dave. "Where's Martha?" *New York Daily News.com*.
March 8, 2004. http://www.nydailynews.com/news/crime_file/
v-pfriendly/story/171479p-149607c.html (November 7, 2005).

"How Martha Coped at 'Yale.'" *CBS News.com*. September 20,
2005. http://www.cbsnews.com/stories/2005/09/20/
entertainment/main860422.shtml (September 25, 2005).

Martha Stewart: It's a Good Thing. New York: A&E Home Video,
2000.

"Martha Stewart Living Omnimedia, Inc. 2003 Annual Report."
Mobular Technologies. 2004. http://ccbn.mobular.net/ccbn/7/
635/684/ (October 29, 2005).

Naughton, Keith. "Martha Breaks Out." *Newsweek*, March 7,
2005, 36–44.

"Oprah's Cut with Martha Stewart." *O, the Oprah Magazine*.
September 2000. http://www.oprah.com/omagazine/200008/
omag_200008_martha.jhtml (November 7, 2005).

The Smoking Gun. Date. http://www.thesmokinggun.com/archive/
stewart.html (November 6, 2005).

Steinhaus, Rochelle. "Liar or Victim of Government
  Overzealousness?" *Court TV.com*, January 28, 2004. http://www
  .courttv.com/trials/stewart/012704_ctv.html (September 25, 2005).
Stewart, Martha. *Entertaining*. New York: Clarkson Potter, 1982.
Thomas, Landon, Jr., and Beth Landman Keil. "Who Knew?" *New
  York*, July 8, 2002. http://www.newyorkmetro.com/news/
  articles/02/marthastewart/index.htm (November 19, 2005).
Toobin, Jeffrey. "Lunch at Martha's." *New Yorker*. February 2,
  2003. http/www.newyorker.com/printables/fact/030203fa_fact
  (September 25, 2005).
Tyrnauer, Matt. "The Prisoner of Bedford." *Vanity Fair*, August
  2005, 110–119, 176–180.

FURTHER READING AND SELECTED MARTHA STEWART MEDIA

Meachum, Virginia. *Martha Stewart: Successful Businesswoman*.
  Springfield, NJ: Enslow, 1998. This book details Stewart's life
  and successful career.
Shields, Charles J. *Martha Stewart*. Philadelphia: Chelsea House,
  2002. Shields details Stewart's life and her commitment to
  her company.
Spinale, Laura. *The Story of Martha Stewart Living*. Mankato,
  MN: Smart Apple Media, 1999. This book examines the
  growth of Stewart's magazine in the context of her personal
  drive and of the popularity of cooking and decorating media.
Entertaining. New York: Clarkson Potter, 1982. Stewart's first
  book remains a classic on home entertaining. Even if the
  reader never intends to prepare an elegant sit-down lunch for
  250 people, the recipes and tips are interesting and inspiring
  to Stewart fans.

Everyday Food. New York: Martha Stewart Living Omnimedia, 2003–2006. This small monthly magazine contains simple (usually one page with a photograph) recipes for entrées, snacks, and desserts. Each recipe comes with complete nutritional information. A link to the *Everyday Food* TV show on PBS is available on *MarthaStewart.com*.

The Martha Rules: 10 Essentials for Achieving Success as You Start, Grow, or Manage a Business. New York: Rodale Books, 2005. As an award-winning TV host, cook, writer, entrepreneur, and self-made billionaire, Stewart has the credentials to offer business advice. In this guide, she explains her top principles for success in any type or size business.

MarthaStewart.com. http://www.marthastewart.com/. Visitors to Stewart's website can search for recipes and craft instructions, watch how-to videos, shop for DVDs, cards, and flowers, and read Stewart's monthly column. The site also includes links to other Martha Stewart Omnimedia publications and to corporate information.

Martha Stewart Living. New York: Martha Stewart Living Omnimedia, 1991–2006. First launched in 1991, Stewart's magazine remains an important part of her media empire. In 2005, 1.8 million people bought *Living*. Each issue contains recipes, craft projects, pet-care tips, gardening ideas, and other home and lifestyle information.

Martha Stewart's Baking Handbook. New York: Clarkson Potter, 2005. From her childhood days of making peach pies with a neighbor, baking has long been one of Stewart's passions. This book includes more than two hundred recipes for breads, cakes, pies, and cookies. Clear instructions are illustrated with how-to photographs and photographs of the finished products.

Weddings. New York: Clarkson Potter, 1987. This early Stewart book documented forty real-life weddings, from a cathedral in Montreal, Canada, to a ranch in Texas. Among the many photos, Stewart offers advice on dresses, invitations, music, and wedding traditions and their meanings. The text also includes recipes and decoration how-to instructions.

INDEX

OTHER TITLES FROM TWENTY FIRST CENTURY BOOKS AND BIOGRAPHY®:

Ariel Sharon
Arnold Schwarzenegger
The Beatles
Benito Mussolini
Benjamin Franklin
Bill Gates
Billy Graham
Carl Sagan
Che Guevara
Chief Crazy Horse
Colin Powell
Daring Pirate Women
Edgar Allan Poe
Eleanor Roosevelt
Fidel Castro
Frank Gehry
George Lucas
George W. Bush
Gloria Estefan
Hillary Rodham Clinton
Jacques Cousteau
Jack Kerouac
Jane Austen
Jesse Ventura
Joseph Stalin
Latin Sensations
Legends of Dracula
Legends of Santa Claus
Malcolm X
Mao Zedong
Mark Twain
Maya Angelou
Mohandas Gandhi
Napoleon Bonaparte
Nelson Mandela
Osama bin Laden
Pope Benedict XVI
Queen Cleopatra
Queen Elizabeth I
Queen Latifah
Rosie O'Donnell
Saddam Hussein
Stephen Hawking
Thurgood Marshall
Tiger Woods
Tony Blair
Vera Wang
V. I. Lenin
Vladimir Putin
Wilma Rudolph
Winston Churchill
Women in Space
Women of the Wild West
Yasser Arafat

ABOUT THE AUTHOR

Ann Kerns has edited many nonfiction books for young readers and is the author of *Australia in Pictures* and *Romania in Pictures*. She enjoys reading, travel, cooking, and music. A native of Illinois, she is a happy transplant to Minneapolis, Minnesota.

PHOTO ACKNOWLEDGMENTS

The images in this book are used with the permission of: © Ron Galella/WireImage.com, pp. 2, 62; © Jeff Haynes/AFP/Getty Images, p. 6; Library of Congress (LC-USF33-003046-M2), p. 10; © Spencer Platt/ Getty Images, p. 12; © Nutley High School/ZUMA Press, p. 20; AP/ Wide World Photos, pp. 22, 58, 90, 102; Barnard College Archives, p. 24; © Keystone/Getty Images, p. 29 (left); © Bettmann/CORBIS, p. 29 (right); © Gail Mooney/CORBIS, p. 32; © age fotostock/Super- Stock, p. 35; © Arthur Schatz/Time Life Pictures/Getty Images, pp. 40, 48, 56; © Stephen Chernin/Getty Images, p. 43; © Susan Wood/Getty Images, p. 54; © John Dominis/Time Life Pictures/Getty Images, p. 64; © David Graham/Time Life Pictures/Getty Images, p. 66; © Supplied by/Globe Photos, Inc., p. 70; © Fitzroy Barrett/Globe Photos, Inc., p. 74 (left); © Gregory Pace/CORBIS, p. 74 (right); © Henny Ray Abrams/AFP/Getty Images, pp. 76, 81; © Richard Lautens/Toronto Star/ZUMA Press, p. 78; © Dave Einsel/Getty Images, p. 82; © Dan Herrick-KPA/ZUMA Press, p. 87; © REUTERS/Chip East, p. 92; © Jeff Zelevansky/Reuters/CORBIS, p. 96; © NBC Universal/WireImage.com., p. 100. Front cover: © Nancy Kaszerman/ZUMA PRESS; Back cover: © Nutley High School/ZUMA Press.